Levels of the Ocean:
The Night Watch of a Sailing Mother

poems by

Magdalena Louise Hirt

Finishing Line Press
Georgetown, Kentucky

Levels of the Ocean:

The Night Watch of a Sailing Mother

Copyright © 2022 by Magdalena Louise Hirt
ISBN 978-1-64662-795-0 First Edition
All rights reserved under International and Pan-American Copyright Conventions. No part of this book may be reproduced in any manner whatsoever without written permission from the publisher, except in the case of brief quotations embodied in critical articles and reviews.

Publisher: Leah Huete de Maines

Editor: Christen Kincaid

Cover Art: Magdalena Louise Hirt

Author Photo: Deborah Schakel

Cover Design: Elizabeth Maines McCleavy

Order online: www.finishinglinepress.com
also available on amazon.com

Author inquiries and mail orders:
Finishing Line Press
PO Box 1626
Georgetown, Kentucky 40324
USA

Table of Contents

Sunlight Zone:

A Caribbean Night Crossing   1

Twilight Zone:

Crossing the North Atlantic from the BVI to Ireland   3

Midnight Zone:

Sailing the Baltic Sea and Motoring the Thames   9

Abyssal Zone:

Crossing the Bay of Biscay   16

Hadal Zone:

At sea between Baiona, Spain, and the Canary Islands   22

Deep Trench:

At Museo Atlántico, Canary Islands   31

Resurfacing:

After reading George Mackay Brown's "Song: Further than Hoy"   35

Sunlight Zone

A Caribbean Night Crossing

Orion

I will be your bowsprit,
your lady between worlds. Anchored
or bobbing on the waves, I will stretch
my arms strong on the front steel
and push my breasts forward
like a wooden god. There, I
can also stretch
back
securing
my buttocks evenly
on the headsail, stretching
my whole torso
to place arms in grip around
the wrapped sail above
and praise you—always.
There. In my mind... and dark sky.

Pull your sword, and I'll strengthen
my bare, calloused feet
on our traveling home.

Call me. To bed, to the depth, to length
and echo me through Homer's
past, where life, blood, belt, and body
were memorized
and most important moist tongues
told truths.

Call me. Just.
Call me... I'm listening.

To dust. To ground. To touch.
To splash, move, groove, cut, split, dive...
To nothingness. To everything. To you.

Water. Orion. Stars—Fish.
Floating parallels. Me
and you.

Twilight Zone

Crossing the North Atlantic
from the BVI to Ireland

Waves that will Swallow Your Heart

Threaten me with your huge size approaching, then pick up
my aft and make it move. You come
repeatedly in different sizes nonstop. I have no
control. White caps, squalls, water
over the bow splashes through my hatches. Screams
from underneath. Eyes fill
with brilliant sapphire deepness.

Moon Trail on the Water

The sea
is quiet tonight, talking
only with small curves. She calls me
to walk the moon trail promising a safety
she cannot provide. The waning moon's smile
teases me, makes fun of me with an eerie laugh
Keeping secrets. Below the surface, he stares
at me, Triton, knowing my vulnerability. A curve
of a wave swells from the deep. It whispers
to me to bend my will, then decides, "No, I'll save her
for later." Clouds saunter in and the ocean
goes black. More calls I hear, spirits, waiting
and wondering about me. The stars, unglamorous
tonight, peep through holes judging. Sails
bang. The ocean whispers. Phytoplankton
lights up as currents hit the hull squeaking
at me, chirping. The bioluminescence glows,
blinks, winks, and whispers
to my sails. Behind us,
our own trail
of fantasy
dust
lingers
for you
to follow.

Wind

Wild. It caresses my face
under the stars. Harnessed.
It gives us wings to fly
down the swells of the Atlantic.
It is the in-between element.
The mystery of space between
surface water tension and stars.
It is a powerful god like the sea.
Granting us distance and swiftly
taking it away. Like a dance, she
circles around us, moves our sails,
slaps our sides with breakers. She
brings the north. Cold. Calling.
With the smell of mossy glens
and Celtic cliffs. She whistles
and howls in one sentence. She
plays with me like a giggling child.
I must chase her laughing. She
pushes, drags, pulls, glides, blows
at me with her every thought. She
holds nothing back. Like an ancestor
filled with knowledge, she is patient
and waits for us to discover our own
strengths side by side. She spins, she
pushes, she is light on her toes.

Caught between Sunrise and Moonset

Soaring on the surface of steel blue
and burnt orange in a blushing dawn.

Crossing

The Sea. Endless rolls of curls that push, slide, coast us to where we've never been. Travel slow. Look to the horizon. Determine the language of the clouds. Feel the wind. Connect your heart to your sails and understand how to hug the power. Think of your destination, but do not let it decide how you embrace your moment, your sail. Sail where wind and waves have an argument, where they dispute your future, and ride the difference, the heat of the conversation. Let the breakers wink at you to share the secret only both of you know: The ocean, the water, our home, is a mystery that we must discover with a bottomless glass of bravery, a thirsty soul for the unknown. See the swells move on from your encounter. Notice how you have changed them, changed yourself, changed what's underneath. Head the opposite direction everyone told you to go. Become what they didn't expect. Live what your eyes always read: distance, adventure, life, thirst.

Cold steel. Harness. Disappearing stars.

late
for my
night shift

Chubby cheeks. Rising chest. Rocking waves.

Baby
Boy
Sleeping

Committed to the Sea

Throw me like a bottle into her arms. Tell the world that I'm lost in throws and thrusts. I'm tossed and turned by her whims, love, and hate. Only her mercy moves me magically across the minimal and maximum. Scotland pulls us relentlessly across danger and mystery. With no choice, our souls tread water and wait and wait and wait. Destination? Journey? Both burn within us, embers that won't ever extinguish. The desire of travel tingles up my legs with an anxious thirst to move. When will she let me go? Never. Move. Move. Move some more. Sail. Sail. Wind. Wind. Water. Move. Swells. Pushes. Pulls. On and on. Time. In my hands. Children. In my hands. Future in our hands. Will our pulls stop in the mossy, mountainous ridges of cliffs or call us further? Cottage by the sea with embers that burn and stay still? Or Selkie skin cherished and never given to a treasure chest to be held and hidden. Swim or stand. LIVE or live? BE or be? LOUD or quiet. Cradle or bed? Brace yourself. Wash your hands. Rid your soul of all the comforts you know. They are not here for you. They live in a memory, a place that you grasp at but does not exist. Water. Life. Sea. Ocean. Expanse. Mess. Nothing written in stone. Always, always moving on.

Lost at Sea

Day seven on the North Atlantic is cold and eerie. At night, a fog rolls in and you feel surrounded in nothingness like the Bermuda Triangle, lost at sea eternally. The days roll in and out with watches and cooking and sailing. Before you know it, the day is dark again and the kids are snuggling into covers with cozy pajamas trying to keep warm. The edge of a storm has been bearing down on us according to the weather updates, but we have not seen it. Gently we roll towards Northern Europe surfing the waves. Our depth finder keeps pinging that we are in six to nine feet deep waters. Something that does not need air is following us below the surface. A wave takes us high to the clouds, and we can see miles, and then we slip down into a deep trough seeing only the next as it approaches. Morale is low key, comfortable. There is excitement slowly growing as we click off the miles. Cliffs, castles, cozy wool sweaters, sheep, land as far as we can see will be in hand soon.

A Fog

Here. In the now. Surrounded by light. Blinded
by moisture. Riding mountains of water
and being tossed like a kid at a playground.

Protected by Ireland

It's all so familiar to me now,
the sea, the ocean. Movement.
The breeze pulls us forward
gently speaking night lullabies.
A half-moon hogs half the sky.
Stars, my constellations, talk on
the other. Mars, closer than ever
before, burns a deep red behind me.
A line clangs on the hollow of the mast.
Waves give me my reliable balance.
The sea. St. George's Channel. Many
wrecks 250 feet below. No battles
tonight. No canons. Souls sleep.
Sunlight rises orange. Time for tea.

Midnight Zone

Sailing the Baltic Sea
and Motoring the Thames

Company
 —*for the 2019 ARC Baltic Rally*

As sunrise smoothly paints
and stretches watercolors,
when the wind is gentle
but the sails bulb full,
when sea deep, wide, and long
water fill the lines and helm
in hand with history,
when the cobalt surface
and the water tension hold
to separate two worlds
and peacefully work them
together, I am sailing
in good company.

The Water Sleeps

The sky wakes and wets
the windows of my cockpit.
The wind is only our own.
Quietly we motor, sail out,
northwest through Swedish
waters. Small adventures
have led us so far from home.
The sky warms. The sea sits.
I ponder words and settle on plain
and simple. Breakfast will come
after others awake still asleep
like the water.

Through the Fog

Like a camper van seeking
refuge in the woods, we motor
on into the darkness with the moon
blurry wandering and seeking us.

The waves motion us up
and down like constant grooves
in a cement path. The lights
of rocks pulse their light

like stop signs at intersections
signaling transition, and we motor
our sailboat through the fog
of the night wondering,

will morning bring destination,
because like being in the fog,
there is no end—only soft
moves that settle on the skin.

North Star

I find you at night staring
with a dim light by tracing
the shoulder of the bear
to the end of your tail.
The poor dragon fights
you every night and never
wins. It cuddles you
and keeps you safe.
Your light tonight is dim
compared to the flashes
of the windmills, the moon,
and the passing boats.
The queen of the sky
outshines you with love
for her king. I wonder
if you think of me
back in my old bedroom,
my childhood bedroom
that led me to you
and back again
as I dreamt safely
in a bed that didn't rock
and sway, tack
and tack again, motor
loud and push
through waves
and lights
and you.

Change the Water
  —*inspired by Walt Whitman*

Like there is water in the ocean, write.
Fill the world with eye-opening words
so that humanity drowns in it. Captain
the ship that saves them swimming
in the storm. Wake them up to care.
Make the waves so big that sailors
get tossed up vertically and recover
with a tack to sail in a new direction.

Windy Nights
  —*inspired by Emily Dickinson, poem 249*

The wind—whistles, slaps
The danger of the wave
The next one—trough
Too narrow

Groans—the Winds—
Strong enough to pin—
Strong enough to trap—
Strong enough to terrify—

Grant me a window—
Oh, let me recover—
Decrease to a whisper—I beg—
But do not disappear

The Bells of the Thames
—inspired by Edgar Allan Poe's "The Bells"

On the Thames, Thames, Thames,
We motor up towards Oxford
To stop here and there to explore
The Thames, Thames, Thames
That never ends. We pass narrow
Boats that moor the winter
On the towpaths of fields.
We join them with kites, bikes,
And drinks on the Thames, Thames,
Thames. We fall asleep in the rain
And dream of being on the Thames,
Thames, Thames. We find our castle,
Our prison, our rental boat, and miss
Selkie on the Thames, Thames, Thames.

Water Heights
—inspired by Emily Brontë's "The night is darkening round me"

A "tyrant spell has bound me" and yet
I move, splash, sail, bob, sway with you
over the seas, dragging my soul unknowably
towards where you want to go, where we
want to be. A life of constant movement.
Souls intertwined spinning over a deep sea.
What pulls me to you, I cannot break. I am
under the magic that made you. Never wanting
release from the highs and lows, ebbs
and flows, crests and troughs—I am hitched.

Abyssal Zone

Crossing the Bay of Biscay

Summertime Perhaps

The wind still comes from the north,
which makes my bones ache with chill
that I can't shake, but I look at the birds
differently now—how they fly in the light—
up, down, up, down, touching and landing
on the water here and there—confused,
perhaps themselves wondering
on the weather. Locals swim early
in the morning—a ritual to wake the spirit,
perhaps. I squeeze into a full wetsuit,
my sealskin—flippers and snorkel—I take deep
breaths to acquire the strength for the temperature.
The English Channel water life can thrash you into
a quick submission—it does not rest in the summer—
perhaps upset too that the gray clouds won't share
the sun. A dolphin with a scar on its back
from a propellor flies with us—pulled by the chirps
and squeals of my young girls' voices. It comes close
to spray us as it breathes and scratches its worries
along our anchor chain. Steel blue waters laugh
at my need for warmth. I pull in the head sail—
not enough wind at the moment. I bury my face
into my scarf making new decisions
about the meaning of July.

Night Sky

Venus, Saturn, Jupiter, and Mars
all seen with the naked eye
drifting, sailing, motoring
forward. The stars light up
the sea tonight. Calm, she
lets me pass the English
Channel. Venus is a bright,
little, piercing light that casts
her own reflection. Saturn
twinkles small and dips behind
clouds. Jupiter, bold and big,
so far away, glares me down
with a proud amber glow
that dares me to watch. Mars
is a sidekick that keeps me
company. The northern
constellations that always
bobbed off my bow are behind
me. The cosmos, like the sea,
are gentle. Some combination
has given me permission to pass.

Trying to Sleep

Clouds roll in and cover
the light of the moon. Squalls,
thunderstorms in the darkness
keep the captain busy. Lines in,
sails in, lines out, sails up sound
like gods fighting from below. With two
of my four children, I lay awake. Our boat
heels port, but not too strong. There is still
up-down, back and forth as we sail
through Biscay. I wake the kids
to move sideways in the bed to keep
pillows high and room for our souls
to drift back asleep, but I lay awake.
I've lost this fight in this cradle for rest.

Sunrise

The freighters rush towards us,
huge cities, locusts, hungry to swallow
a wee sailing vessel. We dodge and weave
as the horizon turns a bright orange
and pray friendly captains hold the helms.
"Fuck you, you French asshole" is heard
on the VHF, then "Quack, quack, quack!"
Whatever that means. We sail through it
seven knots in a fifteen-knot wind. Container
ships, ten high and twice as wide, come close
enough to kiss us. A land breeze keeps
the ocean flat as we approach the dreaded
shelf of the Bay of Biscay, 662 feet will deepen
to 9,849. Waves that sink boats wait there.
The sky lightens to a lavender blue. Only
the creaks of lines and whips of wind
tell me my future on the uneven sea.

Jupiter & Saturn Portal

Darkness. Like flying through space,
I motor through the night, sails tucked
in—no wind. A fisherman, off port
bow, a mile out, keeps my attention.
I pat my hand around the cushions
of the cockpit to find the heavy, black,
strong binoculars. My monitors say
we might collide, but I see his dim lights
blinking out of the way. Straight ahead
my portal awaits. Saturn and Jupiter
aligned on an angle straight ahead
like my sailing vessel would finally hit
that horizon in the distance and float
off into outer space, and then they
disappear, and I am left bobbing,
motoring under all the other questioning
stars gathered in their constellations
keeping their distant secrets. Fishing
vessel, Peixino, is working the shelf,
northern Spain, Bay of Biscay. His wife
is home in bed dreaming, while I, in
my Musto bibs, tumble forward under
a shooting star that crosses over
Peixino and under Mars. I make
a wish—it's always for safe passage,
gentleness of the sea, healthy & happy
children tucked in bed rocking
to the waves. Behind me, Venus appears
brightly contending my portal
shimmering like my past northern
memories. Direction cosmos—unknown.

Hadal Zone

At sea between Baiona, Spain
and the Canary Islands

Portuguese Waters

Like Pablo Neruda, "Tonight
I can write the saddest lines."
Torture, sickness, distance
too far to hold, I scrub puke
out of the couch and clothes
while my four-year-old apologizes
over and over like the waves that come
again and again. I comfort him and let him
know it is okay. I, myself, want to die, cry,
turn around, stop, but that is not possible.
Back and forth, bang, clang, argh, it's
too hard. Where's the parachute?
Only in sleep will I find release, so I close
my eyes and beg for land that holds still.

These Stars

no one
sees them
but me

Darkness that Moves

a creepy
sea monster
it needs
no tentacles
no jaws
no claws
its mystery
movement
and darkness
communicates
grasp
thirst
control
of me

Bang, Clang

The night sparkles above and below
tonight teeming with life and mystery.
Bang, clang, creak, hull smash,
wave break, whomp goes the sail.
Wind behind us, waves to quarter,
we surf over thousands of creatures.
Bang, clang, creak, hull smash,
wave break, whomp goes the sail.
Up, down, stars, sea, up, down,
open ocean. Portugal off port side.
Bang, clang, creak, hull smash,
wave break, whomp goes the sail.
Sailing is flying through darkness
back and forth changing my pattern.
Bang, clang, creak, hull smash,
wave break, whomp goes the sail.
My children dream of far-off places
forgetting they are above the deepest.
Bang, clang, creak, hull smash,
wave break, whomp goes the sail.
The vessel Max Stability approaches
and I giggle at the irony of the surface.
Bang, clang, creak, hull smash,
wave break, whomp goes the sail.

The End

Do you know what it's like to think you are gonna die? To feel yourself fall in the dark and say this is it? When the boat creaks like the inside of a falling tree, and the waves smack from a random squall? Do you know what it is you find important? What you would say to yourself? Or what you wish you would have said to someone else? Who do you wish to be holding in that moment? Will you be satisfied with the life you've had? Will you be able to deal with the fact you've sailed your whole family out to the vast, deep, terrifying ocean and there is nothing you can do to change that? Do you know what it's like to be gripped by nightmares and things banging and falling apart? I've had that kinda night, but it was all in my head. I awoke for my shift to a gentle breeze bobbing us slowly along the lapping waves—in a dark paradise.

Rest at Sea

so important
to happiness
the boat
the weather
the wind
the waves
the connection
between you
and the planet
either rock
you to sleep
or jolt you
rip you
tear your night
into shredded
pieces
like a worn out
shredded flag
with no replacement
that is kept
whipping
used
slowly disappearing
on the stays
unless
you rest
then the night
holds
comfort
wonder
calling
peace
quiet

Darkness Routine

Dinner is done. Drowsy Dramamine too. I pull the covers
of my own bed up on my two girls and kiss them
goodnight wishing on the hull and strong aft of Selkie,
our sailing home, to keep them safe. Off the coast of Africa,
moving through the vast ocean at sunset, I make my husband
a cup of coffee and a cup of tea before I kiss him goodnight
and say, "Be safe. Keep us safe. I love you." I crawl into
the bottom bunk with my youngest son. Squeezed together
cuddling, we hold tight and talk about the others and how far
we have yet to go. We wedge pillows on either side of us (port hull
and leecloth) to make the rocking back and forth bearable
for our bodies to rest and sleep to come. Meanwhile, my oldest son,
takes care of his dad. He asks him questions, learns some sailing,
tells some jokes, and suggests some movies. I believe he worries
and admires his dad to the point of heartache. Then, before he climbs
into the top bunk above me, he leans in for a kiss, a goodnight,
an "I love you," and a short mess of his brother's hair. Sleep comes,
but not without waking, little whines, and knocking of loose items
during erratic waves. Then it's my turn to hover over all from the cockpit,
watching the wind, noting the boats, feeling the waves. Never before
have I felt so close to outer space. I could be anywhere sailing—flying—
drifting through anything. Such deep darkness gives to these swells
that are impossible to see. Each one surfs you up to float weightless
and then drops you hard sideways to remind you of the gravity.
Check the instruments, trust the instruments, adjust the instruments.
Six knots into complete black. These stars, over Africa, Morocco, and me,
have never called my name. Circle. Barrel roll. Sail. A visitor. Always
a visitor. A wave crests white in the darkness, then slips under.
This abyss. How is this possible. Like vulnerable, changeable light,
I breathe in the new, the movement, perhaps changing a few who listen.

Autopilot

The northern constellations
once overhead are hidden
by the horizon. A dust, humidity,
and cloud dim the night stars. Only
Cassiopeia and Taurus stare
at me. The ocean rises but does not
swallow us as we drift through
the night. Alone in the cockpit,
there is a low glow from the instruments
and then darkness beyond my bubble.
No moon, no sun, just wind and water
keep me company. The helm goes back
and forth on autopilot keeping
our course. The manual steering
is out, so I am merely an attentive
bystander on this sailboat's journey.
A strange ghost has his hands
on her. He says nothing and we sit
in comfortable silence sailing.

Strange Embrace

closer to land
a day out
fifth day at sea
you accept it
the giant waves
that break towards you
possibly swallow you
that push you back and forth
hands always in use
in the cabin
one foot there
a knee or hip there
gravity pulling and pushing
you accept it
the movement
the uncertainty
the strange comfort
of life this way
no alternatives
land
day eight at sea
near it
we turn
invisible in the dark
one mile off
six hours
sunrise
anticipation
anxiety
once adjusted
to the sea
it grips you
calls you
wants to keep you
will miss you
holds you
in a strange
embrace

Deep Trench

At Museo Atlántico, Canary Islands

Scuba

Hold your mask, hold your belt,
let the weight of the tank pull you back

to the pillow of the ocean's undersurface. Float,
swim, relax towards the buoys that mark

the beginning. Release the air in your vest
and sink hand over hand equalize down

the line. Others find freedom and magic
as they drop into crystal, clear blue. You

find panic, pressure, uncertainty, torture
that you must breathe slowly through

to survive. Buoyancy. Bottom. Breathe.
Don't panic. Others will find zen. You

will find a mysterious terror. Permission
to enter the sea, only your body fights

itself. The ocean welcomes, swallows.
Explore. Follow the others. There's no

turning back. You want to breathe more,
faster—no. You're in over your head.

Movement will bring the only peace,
so, you breathe, gently swish your legs

and the forward motion is natural. Pause,
float, gaze about, scuba bubbles rise, fish

are curious. First statues are children
going to school by canoe. You become

a child like them ready to learn, vulnerable.
Then the immigrant rib filled with hope

and hopelessness, life and death. Sunken
there, frozen in time, you think of yourself

as one of them, all the souls that rest
on the bottom sand, small creatures crawling

in and out, day and night, calms and storms, pass
overhead. A faceless couple in statue form take

a selfie. Emotionless. Void of sympathy.
Are you like them? A statue under the seaweed?

You try to look them in the eyes to confront
them—there's no eyes to see. Breathe.

Move. You are vulnerable. See the stacks
of cement sticks, barely piled high. They speak,

stack. Last stick, last purpose, repetitive
society—expectations towards death.

You tell yourself, you are not part of the wheel,
you will do it differently, you are now. Then the calm

comes, the steady breath, the wonderment, awe, until
you see the sleepwalkers surrounded by brilliant, sparkling

fish— like confetti, the fish swim in unison around the oblivious.
Why can't they see that they walk to the wall, thoughtless,

towards the point of no return, which you repeat in your head, over
and over with a panic that takes your breath away. Breathe.

Pass through the gate ungracefully worried about the fall,
the awakening, that will come too late—see the apocalypse,

plant people, cactus legged, branch-thorned, growing in the sea. Stop.
Truly see yourself. See the world—see the rich on their playgrounds

of oil money, the six men that bleed the earth. Swinging, stealing,
raping, ruining, what she has only lent. You approach the vortex—

humans swirl naked in a circle: your life, your past, your encounters—
is it your tempest? your compass? your stillness? It's over. Decompress.

Swim slowly up. Pause. Breathe. Don't panic. Don't feel
gutted like a fish, exposed, traumatized, tossed back into

the sea swirling with the life that remains. What can you do?
You open your mouth above the surface—and hear your voice.

Resurfacing

After reading George Mackay Brown's
"Song: Further than Hoy"

Undercurrent of Love

If the "mermaids whisper
through ivory shells a-babble
with vowels" perhaps their language
seeps through the hull into dreams
my girls swim within their sleep. If
"Love walks, alone" perhaps it floats
better off the sea like sound, an echo
over the surface to their small ears
that lay gently bobbing on dry pillows. If
the "hushed awakening" drifts past Hoy,
south of Orkney, past "the hermit's cave
under the mountain" through locked land
canals around orcas waking boats,
it could come to my beauties like sheets
drying in a warm breeze, "further than
song" can rustle branches, glisten
on the water, and shape their whispers.

www.ingramcontent.com/pod-product-compliance
Lightning Source LLC
LaVergne TN
LVHW041556070426
835507LV00011B/1106